THE SECOND WORLD WAR IN THE AIR
IN PHOTOGRAPHS

1940

L. ARCHARD

AMBERLEY

Acknowledgements

All images are courtesy of Campbell McCutcheon unless otherwise stated.

First published 2014

Amberley Publishing
The Hill, Stroud
Gloucestershire, GL5 4EP

www.amberley-books.com

British Library Cataloguing in Publication Data.
A catalogue record for this book is available from the British Library.

ISBN 978 1 4456 2239 2 (print)
ISBN 978 1 4456 2262 0 (ebook)

Typesetting and Origination by Amberley Publishing.
Printed in Great Britain.

Introduction

The New Year of 1940 started as 1939 had ended, with the Phoney War still in full swing. Luftwaffe aircraft continued to carry out attacks on British targets, including shipping in the North Sea (to protect against Luftwaffe attacks, trawlers were armed with turrets carrying twin Lewis machine guns), and the first German aircraft was shot down over England (a Heinkel He 111 bomber intercepted over Whitby). On the part of the RAF, offensive activity in the first months of 1940 was largely limited to continued leaflet raids over central Europe. Bomber Command would suspend the leaflet campaign in April 1940, but not before its crews had flown missions as far as Vienna, Prague and Warsaw.

Most of the aerial activity during the early part of 1940 was happening as part of the Winter War between Finland and the Soviet Union. The beginning of 1940, surprisingly, saw Finland holding the upper hand as Soviet forces became bogged down. However, superior Soviet resources, including the use of air power, began to tell. The Soviets had bombed civilian targets in Finland from the beginning of the war, in November 1939, and this continued into 1940. Soviet air power was also used to support ground troops as they moved forward into Finland. The Winter War would officially come to an end following a ceasefire that came into effect at 11 a.m. on 13 March; early that morning, the Soviet air force carried out one last bombing raid.

Although action was limited to a relatively small number of pilots, the RAF was not standing still during the first months of 1940. In January, the Women's Section of the Air Transport Auxiliary delivered its first aircraft from factory to depot in a widening of the participation of women in the British war effort; meanwhile, Polish pilots who had escaped the devastation of Poland's air force during the German invasion were serving both in the RAF and in the Free Polish forces in the hope of being able to carry on the fight.

Signs that they would not have to wait long started to appear in March. The first civilian death in an air raid on Britain in the Second World War came that month when a man was killed in an attack on the Scapa Flow naval base in Orkney on 17 March. The RAF retaliated with a raid by fifty bombers on the German seaplane base at Hornum on the island of Sylt, in the North Sea, very close to the German border with Denmark. However, events would really begin to move in April. At the start of the month, Hitler had fixed the date of the German invasion of Denmark and Norway at 9 April and ordered preparations to begin.

Admiral Raeder, the German naval commander, had been explaining the significance of Norway as a base, but it was information that Britain was planning to lay a minefield in Norwegian waters in an attempt to limit German access to Swedish iron ore that persuaded Hitler to order the invasion. Although the German invasion force was largely landed from the sea, the Luftwaffe played a key role, neutralising Norwegian coastal defences at Christiansand and Oslo, where paratroopers captured the airport, allowing reinforcements and air support to be brought in. The British and French troops who were landed in the north of Norway were not prepared for the close co-operation between the Wehrmacht and the Luftwaffe. Meanwhile, the Royal Navy discovered that its ships could not safely operate in coastal waters within range of enemy bombers; for example, the cruiser HMS *Suffolk* shelled Sola airfield, near Stavanger, on the Norwegian west coast, and was then herself damaged in an air attack.

One side effect of note which came from the German invasion of Denmark was the occupation by British troops of Iceland on 10 May. The island had been part of a union with Denmark since 1918, and a Danish dependency for more than a century prior to that. Although far from the fighting in Europe, Iceland would prove to be of great strategic value in keeping control of the North Atlantic.

On 30 April, believing that the Scandinavian campaign was over, Hitler ordered his generals to make their final preparations for the attack against Western Europe. On 10 May, the assault began. As well as carrying out close air support for troops on the ground, German air power was used to mount two large-scale airborne assaults on the first day of the offensive, in Belgium and the Netherlands. In Belgium, German troops, landed from gliders, mounted an attack against the key fortress of Eben Emael, successfully overwhelming the defenders. In the Netherlands, meanwhile, German paratroopers occupied airfields around The Hague as part of a plan to seize the Dutch queen, although they were not successful.

As well as these assaults by German airborne troops, the noteworthy event of the air war over the Low Countries was the Luftwaffe's infamous bombing of Rotterdam on 14 May. The Germans could not relieve part of their airborne forces without passing through Rotterdam; an ultimatum for surrender was issued to the city's defenders, but they played for time. In the confusion over deadlines for the city's surrender, the German ground forces were halted but the Luftwaffe were not. The result was that the city centre was razed to the ground in what has been described as a deliberate act of terror (although the Nuremberg Tribunal after the war ruled the attack militarily justified).

Meanwhile, the RAF was being forced by circumstances to adapt very quickly. The Westland Lysanders, which had been specifically designed for army support, proved so inadequate that the aircraft were withdrawn almost immediately following the German offensive. Similarly, the RAF's Gloster Gladiator fighters proved unable to catch the Luftwaffe's bombers, let alone German fighters; the two Gladiator squadrons survived little more than a week before being sent back to Britain having suffered heavy losses. The Advanced Air Striking Force's Bristol Blenheim and Fairey Battle bombers suffered heavily as well from the air cover given to the German advance. Only two of nine Blenheims returned from a mission on 12 May, and of a force of five Fairey Battles sent to attack the bridges over the Albert Canal, none returned.

As well as Gladiators, the RAF had deployed Hawker Hurricanes to France with the BEF, but not Spitfires. The heavy losses suffered by the squadrons in France made the government reluctant to commit further forces, so the first the Germans would see of the Spitfire was over the beaches of Dunkirk.

Although the Luftwaffe had played an extremely effective part in the German war effort until then, Dunkirk marked the point at which Göring began to overreach himself. Hitler, concerned that the Wehrmacht's lines of communication were overstretched, agreed to a proposal from Göring that the Luftwaffe should be allowed to destroy the Allied forces in the Dunkirk pocket from the air while the Panzers were rested and infantry support was brought up. To protect against the Luftwaffe's attacks, the RAF provided fierce air cover. In *Blood, Tears and Folly* Len Deighton writes that the Luftwaffe's Fliegerkorps II's war diary recorded more aircraft lost on 27 May than in the previous ten days of fighting. However, the RAF's tactic of intercepting Luftwaffe bombers (flying from their bases in Germany) some 20 miles before Dunkirk meant that the beleaguered troops on the beaches saw little air cover and many survivors would complain about this on their return.

The last Allied soldiers were evacuated from Dunkirk on 4 June 1940. However, the fighting in France was not over. Long after Dunkirk, more British and French troops would be evacuated from western and southern France in operations Ariel and Cycle, including on the ill-fated liner *Loncastria*. On the night of 2/3 June, the Luftwaffe bombed Paris, although the city's residents had been warned in advance by leaflets dropped from German aircraft. Despite the warning, some 250 civilians were killed. A new front in the war was opened a week later, on 10 June, when Mussolini declared war on Britain and France, hoping that he would be able to gain a share in the spoils of victory at the last moment. Italy's aerial war began in a way that would quickly become familiar: bombing raids against the strategically vital island of Malta and its British bases. However, RAF bombers retaliated by mounting raids from the south of France against Milan and Genoa; RAF and South African aircraft also attacked Italian bases in North Africa.

The pilots of Fighter Command would not have to wait long for the chance to redeem themselves in the eyes of their critics. On 13 July, Hitler issued Directive No. 15, ordering the Luftwaffe to destroy the RAF and achieve aerial superiority in preparation for the invasion of Britain. The Luftwaffe's initial attacks during July were against convoys in the English Channel. The second phase of the battle began on 12 August; the next day was named Adlertag, or 'Eagle Day', by the German propaganda service and consisted of attacks against ports and RAF airfields in the south-east of England. These first missions were flown from bases in the Pas de Calais region of northern France; from 15 August, Luftwaffe squadrons in Scandinavia would start flying raids against

Britain as well. From August until early September the Luftwaffe kept up the pressure on Fighter Command and its airfields in a battle of attrition, causing heavy casualties. Although Air Vice-Marshal Keith Park (commanding Fighter Command's 11 Group, covering the South East) and Air Chief Marshal Sir Hugh Dowding (commanding RAF Fighter Command) used their resources extremely well, their worst worry, the pilot shortage, seems to have been down largely to poor management by the RAF (for more on this, see Len Deighton's *Blood, Tears and Folly*).

However, seeing no sign that the Luftwaffe was winning the battle of attrition, on 7 September Göring arrived to visit his men in the Pas de Calais and announced a change in tactics. Instead of the RAF airfields, the target was now London. Late in the afternoon of that day, the radar operators reported the largest air raid to date: almost 350 German bombers, escorted by more than 600 fighters. Thanks to the distinctive coastline of the Thames estuary, the bombers were easily able to find their targets in the London docks. Many ships were sunk, and warehouses full of inflammable stores set alight. From that night until mid-November, an average of 160 aircraft attacked London every night, except for when the weather was bad.

There was another big daylight raid on 15 September, which is traditionally seen as the climax of the Battle of Britain. However, the Germans were now concluding that time was against them; Hitler officially postponed the invasion of Britain. As well as the dogged resistance put up by Fighter Command, Bomber Command was regularly attacking the ports along the coast of northern France and the Low Countries where the Germans were concentrating the barges which they hoped to use to transport their invasion force; appropriate barges were hard to find, and it took a long time to get them into position.

On the night of 24/25 August, the Luftwaffe dropped some bombs on London by accident, due to a navigation error. Göring had ordered that London was not to be bombed and was reportedly so furious at being disobeyed that he threatened to post the aircraft captains concerned to infantry regiments. On the following night, the RAF launched a raid against Berlin, but it was cloudy and most of the bombs fell on open countryside south of the city; leading Nazis were unsure if it was a deliberate attack or not and it took several more raids on Berlin to convince Hitler that they were intentional. Nevertheless, it can be argued that this was the start of Bomber Command's programme of nightly bombing raids against German cities – a significant moment in hindsight.

Another significant moment came in September when Hitler inexplicably ordered that German aircraft production should be cut back. Despite this, German technical innovation continued. As the Luftwaffe began their night bombing campaign in the autumn and winter of 1940, they had the same difficulty as Bomber Command would later in the war – how to accurately locate a city centre. At first they adapted Telefunken's Lorenz blind landing system for airliners, which could bring aircraft to within a mile of their target; the X-Gerät system, which was more sophisticated, could pinpoint a specific factory. X-Gerät was used by the Luftwaffe's pathfinder force, Kampfgruppe 100, on the night of 13/14 August to attack the Castle Bromwich Spitfire factory and the Short Brothers factory in Belfast.

As early as mid-May, government scientist R. V. Jones had warned that intersecting radio beams could be used to guide German bombers to their targets, the exact system used by Lorenz and X-Gerät. As more information about the German systems came to light, countermeasures could be developed, although the limits of jamming the signals were exposed when the Germans bombed the industrial city of Coventry on the night of 14/15 November; the jamming was not at quite the right frequency and as a result the Germans were able to filter out the jamming and find their target. The result was a raid so devastating that Joseph Goebbels coined a new word: he described towns that had suffered similar levels of destruction as *coventriert*, or 'Coventried'.

Perhaps the worst night of the London Blitz came right at the end of 1940, on the evening of 29/30 December, when the Luftwaffe changed its target from the London Docks to the City. Heavy use of incendiary bombs created the worst fire since 1666, destroying eight of Sir Christopher Wren's churches. The damage was made worse because a proper system of fire watchers had not yet been put in place, and because of the low level of water in the Thames. The raid lasted for three hours; it had been scheduled to last for nine, but was fortunately cut short by bad weather over northern France.

While the London Blitz was raging, the war in the Mediterranean was starting to gain momentum. On 28 October, Mussolini ordered Italian forces to invade Greece from Albania (which had been conquered by Italy in 1939). The Greeks quickly reacted and by 3 November had gone over to the offensive, pushing the Italians back into Albania. Although General Metaxas, the Greek leader, had been offered the assistance of a British expeditionary force, he had declined for fear that it would provoke German involvement; he did, however, accept the offer of RAF squadrons.

The fighting in Greece was going on at the same time as a campaign against the Italian forces in North Africa, and the war to control the Mediterranean itself. With France out of the war, the Royal Navy would face the formidable Italian fleet alone. In November 1940, Admiral Cunningham, the commander of the Royal Navy's Mediterranean squadron, ordered a daring attack by the Fleet Air Arm. Fairey Swordfish torpedo bombers from the aircraft carrier HMS *Illustrious*, along with five from HMS *Eagle*, attacked the Italian warships anchored in the harbour at Taranto. For the loss of two aircraft, the attack sank three battleships, one of which would never sail again. This daring attack demonstrated that the aircraft carrier was the new key to naval warfare, and other powers were watching: the Japanese assistant naval attaché in London was Minoru Genda, who would later be involved in planning the attack on Pearl Harbor that started the war in the Pacific.

January

An old Fokker CV twin-seat fighter, pressed into service by the Finns against the Soviet attack.

A captured Soviet bomber, taken into the Finnish air force and used against the Soviet forces.

Wide-ranging attacks were carried out against Finnish towns by Soviet bombers on 11 January. This photograph shows firefighters in Helsinki trying to combat fires caused in the attack.

Above and right:
Two images showing
barrage balloons
deployed from lighters
moored off the coast.
The balloons were
meant to discourage
German aircraft from
laying magnetic mines.

Left: One of the youngest female pilots of the Air Transport Auxiliary wearing full uniform.

Below: A group of female pilots of the Air Transport Auxiliary in flying kit, preparing to go on duty.

Leaflets being loaded aboard a Whitley bomber of the RAF prior to a night reconnaissance and propaganda mission over Prague and Vienna.

A group photo showing some of the RAF aircrew who flew on the mission to Prague and Vienna.

These two images show the East Dudgeon lightship, attacked and machine-gunned by Luftwaffe aircraft on 29 January 1940, and the Trinity House vessel *Reculver*, also attacked by Luftwaffe aircraft.

February

The first German plane shot down over England: a Heinkel He 111 bomber brought down by RAF fighters over Whitby.

Another Heinkel 111 brought down over the UK, this time near St Abb's Head in the Scottish Borders.

Firemen in Turku salvaging what they could from a building after the town was attacked by the Soviet Air Force on 17 February.

Above: Bomb damage in the town
of Rovaniemi, which lay on the
railway line north from the Gulf of
Bothnia.

Right: Damage in the village
of Pajala in Sweden, bombed in
error by the Soviet air force. The
Soviets agreed to pay Sweden an
indemnity.

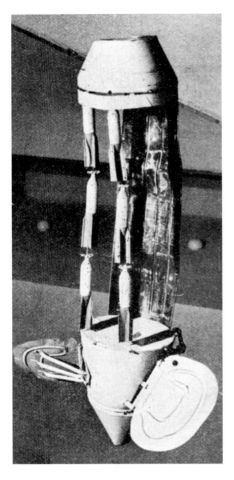

A Soviet air-dropped weapon, containing several small incendiary and high-explosive bombs. These were used in the war against Finland and were known by the Finns as 'Molotov bread baskets'.

The RAF Coastal Command pilots who spotted the *Altmark* while on patrol. *Altmark* was trying to return to Germany through Norwegian waters after a voyage from the South Atlantic carrying prisoners taken by the pocket battleship *Admiral Graf Spee*.

General Sikorski reviewing a unit of the Free Polish air force.

A Polish priest holding a service for members of the Free Polish air force.

Britain's Air Minister, Sir Kingsley Wood, inspecting Polish personnel serving with the RAF.

A turret with twin Lewis guns mounted on board the trawler *Starbank*.

A rather hazy image of German aircraft circling to attack a trawler in the North Sea.

A closer view of the twin Lewis guns, this time aboard the collier *Chatwood*.

The minesweeper HMS *Sphinx* after having been hit by bombs from German aircraft. She later sank while being towed towards port.

The first battle squadron of the Royal Canadian Air Force arrived in Britain on 25 February. They are seen here later in the year being inspected by the Canadian High Commissioner.

Towards the end of February, the merchant ship *Sea Venture* was attacked and sunk by a U-boat. The seaplane partially seen here alongside one of the ship's boats drove the U-boat away and directed a lifeboat to the survivors.

Dusk on a bomber field. Crew members gather around their Armstrong-Whitworth Whitley in preparation for a night reconnaissance mission over Germany while another flight of aircraft above is already departing.

March

The British India liner *Domala*, on fire after being attacked by the Luftwaffe in the English Channel on 2 March 1940. Despite being ablaze, *Domala* was eventually brought into Southampton.

The British ship *Barnhill*, bombed by the Luftwaffe off the South Coast; she remained ablaze for several days.

Plumes of water can be seen in this photo, thrown up by bombs dropped during a Luftwaffe attack on this convoy off the Flanders banks, between Cap Griz Nez (west of Calais) and the Dutch border.

Aircraft of the French air force. Above is an American-built Douglas DB-7 bomber, and below is a French-made Morane 406 fighter.

The results of the last Soviet air raid in the war against Finland, carried out early on 13 March 1940; the ceasefire between Finland and the Soviet Union would come into effect at 11.00 that morning.

A German air raid on the naval base at Scapa Flow in the Orkney Islands on 17 March led to seven casualties at the base and damage to five cottages in the village of Bridge of Waith.

RAF aircrew on their return from the raid on the German base at Hornum on the island of Sylt. The raid was carried out in retaliation for the German raid on Orkney.

Part of the defences of the island of Sylt: one of the many searchlights around the coast.

April

Douglas Bader, who returned to flying fighters with the RAF, posing with some of the pilots in his Canadian fighter squadron. Bader is fourth from the right.

Early in April 1940,
Bomber Command
suspended leaflet raids
over Germany, having
dropped 65 million. These
two images show (*left*)
propaganda leaflets being
loaded onboard a Whitley
bomber and (*below*) the
act of releasing the leaflets
through a chute in the
back of the aircraft.

A Luftwaffe Junkers Ju 52 transport over Norway, transporting material as part of the first wave of the invasion. (*Signal*)

The town of Elverum, where King Haakon of Norway and his staff moved after the attack on Oslo, after being bombed by the Luftwaffe.

German troops on Stavanger airfield; they are thought to be leaving to take up strategic positions. Stavanger airfield was one of the main bases used by the Germans to land troops.

Luftwaffe personnel resting alongside a Stuka dive bomber at Stavanger airport. Heavy air support was a key factor in the speed of the German advance in Norway.

Above: A photograph of Stavanger airfield being bombed by the RAF. In the lower right-hand corner, there are several large bomb craters.

Right: An interior view of one of the German transport aircrafts used to rush reinforcements to Norway after the initial invasion.

An aerial photograph of the southern Norwegian coast near Kristiansand; a 10,000-ton German merchant ship that had been attacked while unloading troops and supplies can be seen on fire in the top left-hand corner.

An aerial photograph showing an attack on German supply ships in a fjord near Bergen. A 2,000-ton German vessel can be seen to the right, sunk in shallow water.

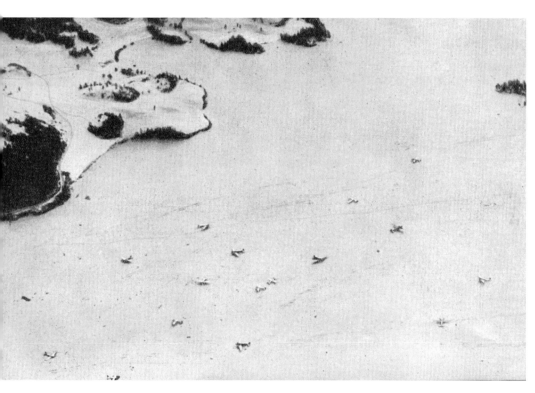

Above: A reconnaissance photograph of a frozen lake, at Jonsvannet, in use as a makeshift Luftwaffe base.

Right: Columns of smoke rising from the port of Aandalsnes following a bombing raid by the Luftwaffe.

Above: Another view showing the results of air attacks on Aandalsnes.

Left: Bomb damage in the city of Trondheim.

Bomb damage in the Norwegian town of Molde.

The RAF attacked supply ships and transports in Hardanger Fjord, near Bergen, on 25 April; warehouses on the wharf can be seen on fire.

Blackburn Skua dive bombers of the Fleet Air Arm. Skuas sank the cruiser *Königsberg* at Bergen, the first major warship to be sunk by air attack in the war.

The cruiser HMS *Suffolk* shelled Sola airfield near Stavanger, but was then herself damaged in an air attack.

On the night of 29/30 April, a German Heinkel He 111 bomber on a minelaying mission crashed at Clacton-on-Sea in Essex. The Heinkel crashed into a garden, burst into flames and exploded, demolishing a complete row of houses and killing two civilians as well as the crew, and injuring 150.

May

Part of Namsos, the port north of Trondheim from which British and French forces were successfully evacuated on 2 May. As can be seen from this photograph, the town was heavily bombed by the Luftwaffe during the evacutation.

Another view showing the very heavy damage inflicted on Namsos during several weeks of bombing raids.

Narvik. This northern Norwegian port was the scene of intense fighting during the Norwegian campaign over April, May and early June 1940 and was heavily bombed.

German reinforcements parachuting into Narvik. This photograph was taken by a German Propaganda Company photographer and published in the magazine *Signal*. (*Signal*)

The Boulton Paul Defiant fighter came into service with Fighter Command in May 1940. Unusually, the Defiant carried its armament in a turret behind the cockpit.

Fairey Battle light bombers being used for training air crew as part of the Commonwealth Air Training Scheme. They are seen passing over the base at Camp Borden in Canada.

On 10 May, the Luftwaffe systematically attacked airfields in France, Belgium and the Netherlands, destroying hundreds of aircraft on the ground, in the first stage of the Blitzkrieg in the west, (*Signal*)

An artist's impression of one of the key parts of the German Blitzkrieg: Junkers Ju 87 Stuka dive-bombers going into the attack.

German paratroopers descend from their transport aircraft somewhere over the Low Countries. German airborne troops occupied airfields around The Hague as part of plan to seize the Dutch capital and kidnap Queen Wilhelmina during the invasion of the Netherlands.

A series of images showing German paratroopers jumping out of their Junkers Ju 52 transport aircraft over the Netherlands, published in the German propaganda magazine *Signal*. (*Signal*)

A German paratrooper by the side of a road in the Netherlands.

German aircraft dropping supplies by parachute to advanced Wehrmacht units in the Netherlands.

These two images, published in the Nazi propaganda magazine *Signal*, show the centre of the Dutch city of Rotterdam after it was attacked by the German Luftwaffe, and (above) German storm troopers in action in the bombed French city of Orléans. (*Signal*)

An RAF pilot clambers into his Fairey Battle light bomber. Five RAF Battle bombers mounted an attack on the bridges over the Albert Canal but all five were shot down.

The bridges over the Albert Canal which were attacked by RAF Battle bombers.

Flying Officer Roland Garland and Sergeant Grey, the crew of the leading Battle bomber to attack the bridges over the Albert Canal, were posthumously awarded the VC.

On 14 May, the Dutch city of Rotterdam fell to German forces after having been heavily bombed; about 980 civilians were killed and nearly 80,000 were left homeless after 20,000 buildings (some two-thirds of the city) were destroyed.

Concerned about Wehrmacht lines of communication being stretched, Hitler agreed to Göring's proposal that the Luftwaffe should destroy Allied forces in the Dunkirk pocket from the air while the Panzers were rested and infantry support brought up at the end of May 1940. This vivid artist's impression shows the BEF rearguard fighting in a French town with a Luftwaffe bomber coming in from the right.

June

Troops on the beach at Dunkirk taking what cover they could as bombs burst in the background.
Despite the RAF's efforts, the Luftwaffe wreaked havoc on the evacuation beaches.

Merchant shipping in Dunkirk harbour, on fire after an intensive Luftwaffe raid.

The aftermath of the Luftwaffe bombing raid on Paris on the night of 2/3 June 1940. The city was attacked by a force of some 200 aircraft but the population had been warned by leaflets dropped by the Germans the night before.

On 10 June 1940, convinced that the war would end soon with a German victory, Italian dictator Benito Mussolini, seen here to the right, reviewing a military parade, declared war on Britain and France. He hoped for a seat at the negotiating table at the end of the war, and a share of the spoils in the Mediterranean.

Above: Italian air force Savoia-Marchetti three-engined bombers.

Right: Civilians on Malta take cover in an air-raid shelter. Italy's first blow against Britain was an air raid on the bases on Malta, something that would become very familiar as the war continued.

RAF and SAAF aircraft attacked Italian bases in Libya, then an Italian colony, in retaliation for the raid on Malta. These two aerial photographs show attacks in progress against Italian airfields.

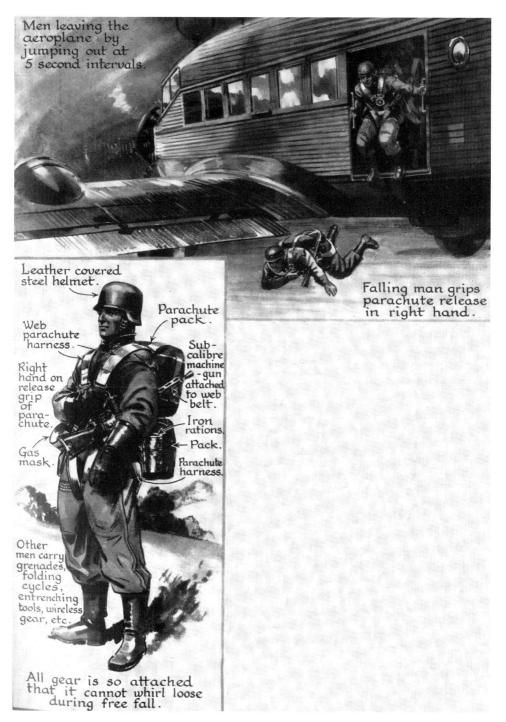

Men leaving the aeroplane by jumping out at 5 second intervals.

Falling man grips parachute release in right hand.

Leather covered steel helmet.

Parachute pack.

Web parachute harness.

Sub-calibre machine-gun attached to web belt.

Right hand on release grip of para-chute.

Iron rations.

Pack.

Gas mask.

Parachute harness.

Other men carry grenades, folding cycles, entrenching tools, wireless gear, etc.

All gear is so attached that it cannot whirl loose during free fall.

These two drawings from *The Illustrated London News* show Soviet paratroopers; Soviet military exercises in 1936 were thought to have inspired the development of the German parachute forces, which in turn inspired Churchill to order a corps of British paratroopers to be trained.

The Cunard liner SS *Lancastria*, attacked and sunk by the Luftwaffe in St Nazaire harbour on 17 June. *Lancastria* was evacuating British troops and civilian refugees from southern France, and about half of the 9–10,000 aboard her at the time of the attack were killed.

A Dornier Do 17 over the island of Guernsey. The Channel Islands were bombed on 28 June and two days later a reconnaissance pilot landed at the deserted Guernsey airfield; as a result of this pilot's report a platoon of Luftwaffe soldiers were landed on Guernsey that night.

Italo Balbo, seen when he was Mussolini's Minister of Aviation in 1929. Balbo made his name as an aviator in the 1920s. In 1933 he was made Governor General of the Italian colony of Libya, and when war broke out he was Commander in Chief of the Italian forces in North Africa. In June 1940, while flying over the Libyan port of Tobruk, Balbo was shot down and killed by Italian anti-aircraft guns. (LoC)

July

Bombs bursting around a convoy under attack in the English Channel from Junkers Ju 87 dive-bombers escorted by Bf 109 fighters. The churning of the water from fragments of shrapnel is visible. Air attacks on convoys in the Channel were the first parts of the German campaign to establish air superiority.

The use of paratroopers in the German invasion of the Low Countries caused a great deal of concern in Britain in the summer of 1940; this illustration shows a range of ways to obstruct potential landing grounds for troop-carrying aircraft.

An aerial photograph showing an RAF attack on what was then Schiphol aerodrome, just outside Amsterdam. A salvo of bombs can be seen exploding at the left of the image.

The scale of the response to Lord Beaverbrook's appeal for aluminium pots and pans to build aircraft can be seen here. Beaverbrook, the Canadian-born owner of the *Daily Express* and other newspapers, was the first Minister for Aircraft Production.

Left: Lord Beaverbrook.

Below: On 24 July, the Italian air force attacked a British base at Haifa, in what is now Israel. Smoke can be seen billowing up from damaged oil tanks in this photograph.

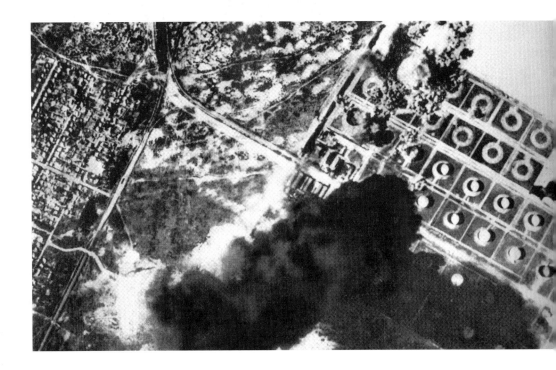

1. Vickers Wellington bombers. During 940, the Wellington was one of the mainstays of Bomber Command, flying missions to drop propaganda leaflets over Germany and later bombing missions.

2. Junkers Ju 87 Stukas flying low over snowy Norway. Stukas played a key role in providing close support to the troops on the ground.

Left and below:
3. and 4. German paratroopers being dropped over northern Norway. There was fierce fighting around the port of Navik, from where the Allied forces were eventually evacuated, and in the mountainous terrain this was the most effective way for Germans to reinforce troops.

Above and right: 5. and 6. German paratroopers on the ground in northern Norway.

7. The view from the nose of a Henkel He 111 bomber over Norway. Note the bridge, which has been deliberately wrecked to prevent its use by the invading Germans.

8. A Heinkel He 111 bomber flying over the northernmost point in Europe, Norway's Nordkapp.

Above and right: 9. and 10. German anti-aircraft guns in Norway. Allied aircraft launched regular attacks in a vain attempt to halt the German advance.

Above: 11. A sound detector, used by the Germans to detect the noise of incoming enemy aircraft.

Left: 12. This German map demonstrates the effectiveness of the Luftwaffe in Norway.

13. A Junkers Ju 52 troop carrier over the Netherlands. German airborne troops would play a key role in the assault on the Low Countries, landing by parachute on airfields in the Netherlands and by glider to capture a key fortress in Belgium.

14. Paratroopers jumping over the Netherlands.

Left: 15. A German Paratrooper.

Right: 16. A fllight of Junkers Ju 87 Stuka divebombers over the Western Front.

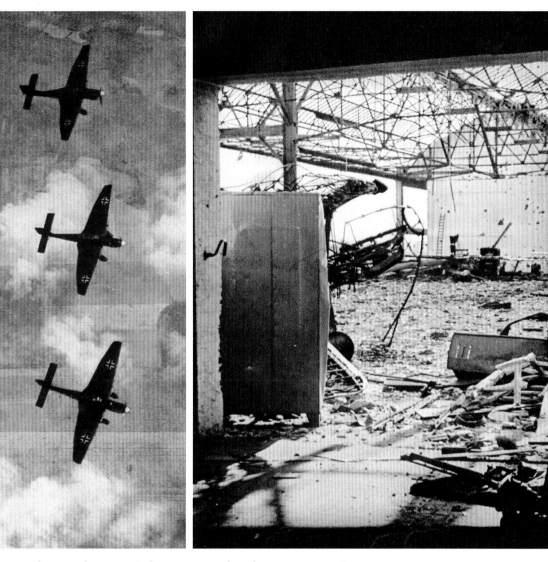

Left: 17. Junker Ju 87 Stukas going into their dive.

Right: 18. The ruins of Charleroi airfield. One of the early parts of the Blitzkrieg on the west was a systematic attack on airfields across northern France, Belgium and the Netherlands.

Above: 19. Light aircraft like this Fiesler Storch were essential for maintaining communications between the forward units of the German Panzer divisions and the troops following up behind.

Left: 20. A German gunner with an 88 mm shell. The German 88 mm gun was formidable as both an anti-tank weapon and an anti-aircraft gun, and would cause heavy casualties among Allied aircraft seeking to disrupt the Blitzkrieg.

21. German gunners racing to man their 88 mm gun as news of an air attack comes in.

22. The wreckage of an RAF aircraft somewhere in France.

23. The French Air Force, too, suffered as a result of trying to counterattack against the German onslaught.

24. Summer 1940 and four Me 109s patrol over the English Channel.

Above: 25. RAF Hurricanes in the air.

Right: 26. A briefing for Luftwaffe air crew, explaining the right course to fly to reach their target.

Left: 27. The tail fin of a Junkers Ju 87 Stuka, marking the missions its pilot has flown over Norway and Britain, and one ship sunk.

Below: 28. Two crews parade in front of a Junkers Ju 88 bomber, which has been loaded with bombs, ready for its next mission.

29. Armourers at a Luftwaffe base prepare amunition for the guns of a Me 110 escort fighter. Designed to have a long range, the Luftwaffe hoped Me 110s would be able to escort bombers to their targets in Britain and back, but the Me 110 was no match for RAF fighters.

30. Wehrmacht personnel studying a map. They are focused on Norway but Britain is not far away.

Air crew of the Italian air force are seen here receiving their final instructions before taking off.

Douglas DB-7 bombers on the assembly line in California. The British mission in the USA was given permission to buy 40 per cent of US aircraft production in July 1940.

On 19 July, the Luftwaffe attacked south-east England; here, bombs are seen exploding in the water off an unnamed harbour, presumably Dover.

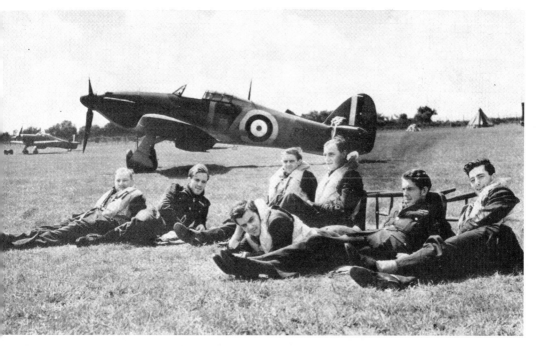

RAF fighters returning to their bases after a battle against the eighty Luftwaffe aircraft which were raiding shipping at Dover and, below, their pilots taking a rest in a classic image of the Battle of Britain and the Few.

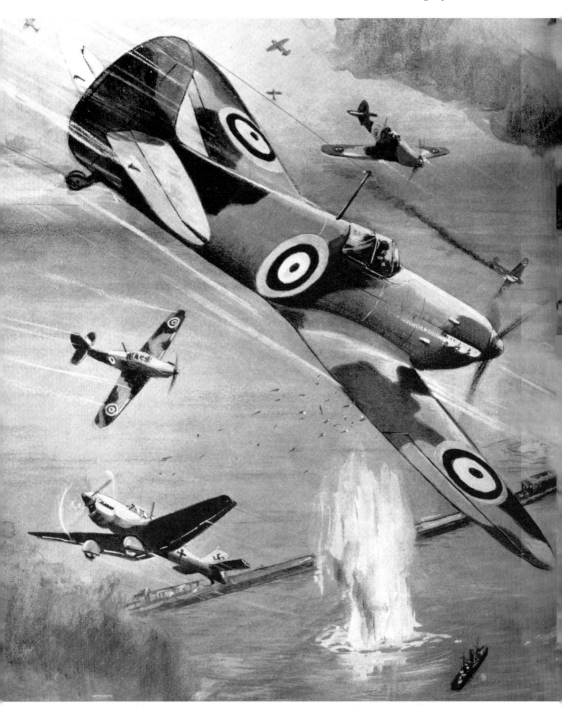

An artist's impression of the fighting over Dover. The Luftwaffe formation consisted of thirty Junkers Ju 87 Stuka dive-bombers protected by fifty fighters. Although the Stukas had been very effective in German campaigns so far, they would not prove to be so during the Battle of Britain.

August

A group of Spitfire pilots sitting on an aircraft wing. August 1940 would see the real start of the Battle of Britain and the legend of the Few.

Dr Edvard Beneš, president of the Czechoslovakian government in exile, reviewing Czech pilots serving with the RAF. Czech pilots and aircrew would play a major part in the Battle of Britain.

King George VI inspecting a Polish squadron of the RAF. Poles, too, would play a key role in the battle.

Two Hurricanes take off from their base to rejoin the battle over south-eastern England, having returned to refuel and rearm.

These two drawings by a German war artist, entitled 'Off to England' (*above*) and 'Over England' (*below*), are an idealised picture of the German attack on Britain.

German aircraft shot down on 15 August, part of a series of raids intended to destroy RAF Fighter Command. The start of this campaign – 'Eagle Day', 3 August – is traditionally seen as the start of the Battle of Britain.

Top and middle: Air power versus sea power in the Mediterranean. The top image was taken from a British warship and shows another ship manoeuvring to avoid Italian bombs, while that to the left was taken from the air and shows an attack on Royal Navy battleships. Mussolini's Italy was attempting to establish superiority in the Mediterranean theatre.

A battleship defending itself against aerial attack with a barrage from quick-firing pom-pom guns. Note the empty shell cases piling up below the guns, and the men with their hands over their ears.

Right: An artist's impression showing two Spitfire fighters circling over the sinking German Heinkel He 111 bomber they have just shot down.

Below: Another aspect of Britain's defences against aerial attack: a barrage of 3.7-inch anti-aircraft guns at night.

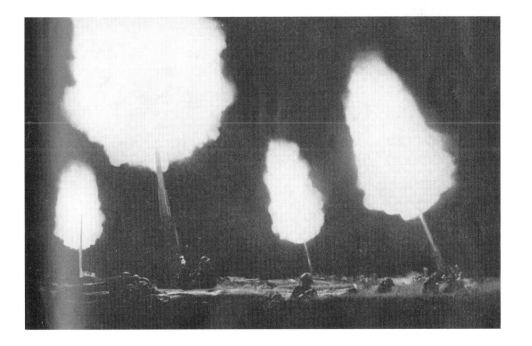

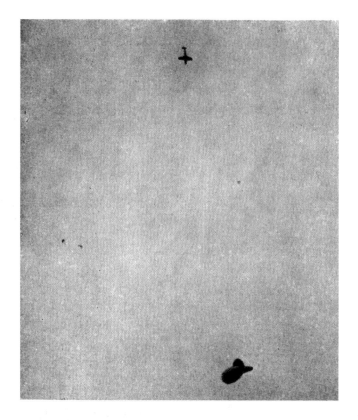

Top and left: Two photographs showing a German Messerschmitt Bf 109 attacking the balloon barrage over Dover.

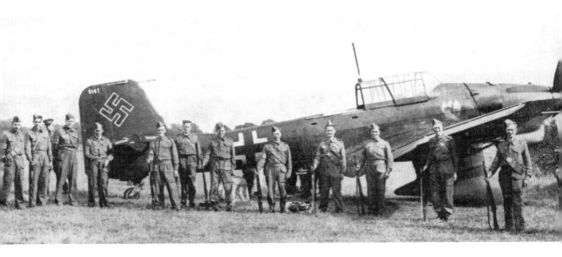

Above: A Junkers Ju 87 Stuka dive-bomber, brought down almost completely undamaged over southern England, surrounded by Home Guard men.

Right: This image shows two barrage balloons falling in flames over the South Coast.

The crew of a Wellington bomber gather around their aircraft after returning from the RAF's first bombing raid on Berlin. Cloudy weather meant that most of the bombs missed the city, and Nazi leaders were unsure whether the attack was deliberate.

Bomber Command aircrew being debriefed by intelligence officers after their raid against

This Heinkel He 111 received three direct hits from anti-aircraft guns, then crashed and destroyed two houses.

Wreckage caused in London by a German attack on the night of 28 August. A mother and three children who had taken refuge in an Anderson shelter were dug out by ARP wardens.

Bomb damage in a London suburb caused on the night of 30 August.

September

Aluminium pots and pans being melted down at a Ministry of Aircraft Production facility. The ministry was struggling to keep Fighter Command supplied with enough aircraft in the face of the German onslaught.

Two German raiders which were shot down in a battle over the Thames Estuary on 3 September; they crashed in Essex, where they are seen being examined.

In an attack on 8 September, this London bus was flung against a nearby building by a bomb blast. Fortunately, the passengers, driver and conductor had all taken shelter elsewhere.

Winston Churchill inspecting bomb damage in central London and the East End.

Tower Bridge silhouetted against the flames of the London Docklands. A big daylight raid on 7 September started the fires, which then acted as a marker for further raids during that night.

The glow of the fires lighting up the Thames and the anchored merchant shipping in the docks.

Above: Debris being cleared from a street in the centre of London. Note the bomb crater to the left of the photograph.

Right: King George V and Queen Elizabeth visiting bomb-damaged areas of the East End of London on 11 September.

Left: A family, bombed out of their own home, shelter in temporary accommodation.

Below: The crew of a Heinkel He 111 bomber, shot down by a Hurricane fighter while returning from a raid on London, are marched away while smoke from their aircraft rises behind.

The crew of a Blenheim bomber wait by their aircraft while the mechanics finish working on it before they set off to attack Italian targets in the Mediterranean theatre.

Smoke rising from the Italian airfield of Neghelli, in what was then Italian East Africa (covering areas of modern Somalia, Eritrea and Ethiopia). A hangar and a Caproni bomber were reported to be hit in an air raid there.

While the Luftwaffe fought to win aerial superiority over the English Channel, concentrations of barges to transport the German invasion force were building up in ports like Le Havre (*above*) in France, and Vlissingen (*below*) in the Netherlands. These were then attacked by RAF bombers.

Another concentration point for invasion barges, attacked by RAF bombers: Dunkirk. Damage caused to the dock buildings by a raid can be seen at the top of the picture.

Left and below: A bomb disposal crew removing unexploded German bombs in London.

Right and below:
Damage caused in Berlin
by retaliatory raids
carried out by the RAF.

An RAF crew disembark from their Wellington bomber after another night raid on Germany.

The trails of German aircraft in the skies above southern England, as they head towards London.

October

On the morning of 8 October, German bombers attacked during London's morning rush hour. Part of the damage can be seen here.

Left: The statue of King Richard I outside the Houses of Parliament; the statue's sword has been bent by a bomb blast, and the window behind blown in.

Below: Londoners sheltering from the Blitz in Aldwych tube station, now closed, near Holborn.

Göring with some of his Luftwaffe generals studying the progress of the campaign against Britain.

Luftwaffe officers gathering at an airfield in northern France to plan the next mission against Britain.

Above: Bombers over Britain; the first puffs of black smoke from anti-aircraft fire can be seen to the right of this photograph.

Left: Roof spotters on duty at a Lancashire mill, to give warning of approaching enemy aircraft in time for the staff downstairs to take shelter.

St Paul's Cathedral with a gaping hole in the roof and rubble over the high altar, caused by a bomb hitting the building; fortunately the bomb didn't explode.

Above: A musical show on the platform at Aldwych tube station for the benefit of the hundreds sheltering there from the bombing.

Left: An office block in London; curiously, the upper floors of the building remained intact.

An anti-aircraft gun crew stockpiling ammunition for the night ahead.

A searchlight crew preparing for another night.

Members of the Eagle Squadron, an RAF unit composed of US volunteers.

Douglas Bader (centre) admiring the artwork on the nose of one of the aircraft in his squadron, composed of Canadian pilots.

A New Zealand crew boarding their Wellington bomber prior to a mission over Germany.

The ruins of the library at Holland House, Kensington, where Joseph Addison (founder of *The Spectator* magazine) and radical Regency politician Charles James Fox had both lived.

The wreckage of a Bf 109 fighter shot down by two Spitfires.

The crew of a shot-down German aircraft are rescued from their inflatable dinghy in the English Channel by a seaplane, part of the Luftwaffe Air-Sea Rescue service. A similar service was in place on the British side of the Channel.

The king and queen visiting bomb-damaged areas of London. The royal family's decision to stay in London during the bombing was very popular.

The evacuation of children away from Berlin, in response to the bombing raids carried out by the RAF.

Left: German aircrew under guard at a railway station in London, on their way to an internment camp.

Below: London trams damaged by bombs in a raid on the morning of 25 October.

In this rather grainy photograph the Canadian Pacific liner *Empress of Britain* is seen under tow after coming under attack by a Focke Wulf C 200 Condor long-range bomber off the coast of Ireland. Hits from two 250-kg bombs started fires that threatened to overwhelm the ship but she was only finally sunk after having been torpedoed by a U-boat while under tow.

Fighter pilots of the Czechoslovak squadron and two RAF officers reading telegrams congratulating them on their performance in battle.

Naples (*above*) and the Škoda works at Pilsen, Czechoslovakia, (*below*) were both targeted for RAF bombing raids at the end of October 1940.

November

An RAF night fighter crew climb aboard their Blenheim Mk IV fighter bomber.

A Hurricane fighter being refuelled while on night operations.

A seventy-year-old man is rescued from the wreckage of a block of flats.

Above: Italian bombers on a raid against a target near Athens. Bombs can be seen falling from the aircraft. Italian forces invaded Greece from Albania at the end of October 1940.

Right: On Armistice Day, 11 November, units of the Italian air force joined the Luftwaffe in attacking Britain. One of the aircrew shot down can be seen under guard in London.

Left: One of thirteen Italian aircraft brought down by the RAF over the Thames Estuary on 11 November. This one crashed near Orford, Suffolk.

Below: Göring addresses a rather sombre gathering at a Luftwaffe base in northern France.

Right: An image by a German war artist showing Luftwaffe bombers over Britain.

Left: Hawker Hurricane fighters deployed to the Western Desert to help fight against the Italians in Libya.

Above: A patrol of Hurricane fighters breaking formation to attack enemy aircraft over the Western Desert.

Left: An artist's impression of a raid by the RAF on Durazzo, on the Adriatic coast of Albania, a key base for supplying the Italian forces which had invaded Greece. Although the Greek leader General Metaxas had declined an offer of a British expeditionary force, he accepted the help of RAF squadrons.

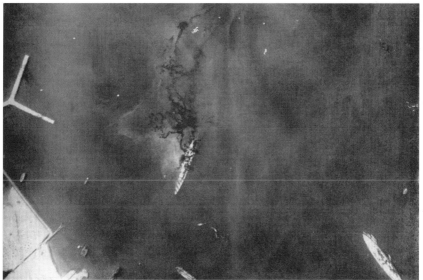

On the night of 11/12 November 1940, Fleet Air Arm torpedo bombers and dive-bombers attacked the Italian fleet at its base in Taranto in a very successful strike. These two aerial reconnaissance photographs show some of the damage inflicted. The top image shows two Trento class cruisers (furthest from the shore) damaged and leaking fuel oil. The image above shows the battleship *Conte di Cavour* with its deck submerged. The Japanese naval attaché in London was very interested in the operation.

An artist's impression of the Taranto attack, Operation Judgement. Flying through a very heavy barrage of anti-aircraft fire, the Fleet Air Arm's Swordfish torpedo bombers knocked out half the Italian navy's capital ships in one night.

A Fairey Swordfish torpedo bomber flying over the aircraft carrier HMS *Eagle*. *Eagle* and its experienced Swordfish pilots were due to carry out the Taranto attack, but a problem with the *Eagle*'s fuel system meant the job was given to pilots from HMS *Illustrious*, assisted by some of *Eagle*'s crews.

Coventry was systematically attacked from the air on the night of 14/15 November 1940, the most devastating of many attacks suffered by the city during the war. The top image shows the ruins of the city's fourteenth-century cathedral, while the image above shows what used to be a busy shopping street in the city centre.

The ruins of a church in Bristol after the city was bombed.

Bomb damage in an unnamed town in the Midlands. The blast has torn away the wall and the floor is tilting down to the ground, but the clock and the other ornaments on the mantelpiece remain undisturbed.

December

Bomb damage to London's Carlton Hotel.

Left and below:
Bomb damage in
Southampton following
heavy raids on the night
of 30 November/1
December.

The wreckage of a school in Liverpool, hit by bombs.

An artist's impression showing RAF bombers attacking retreating Italian troops in the mountains of Greece on 4 December. The campaign in Greece was proving to be a disaster for the Italians.

Above: A Bristol Blenheim bomber returning to its airfield in Greece after a raid on Italian forces, now retreating through Albania.

Left: An aerial photograph showing bombs exploding in the port of Valona, along with Durazzo, one of two ports in Albania used by the Italians to supply their forces.

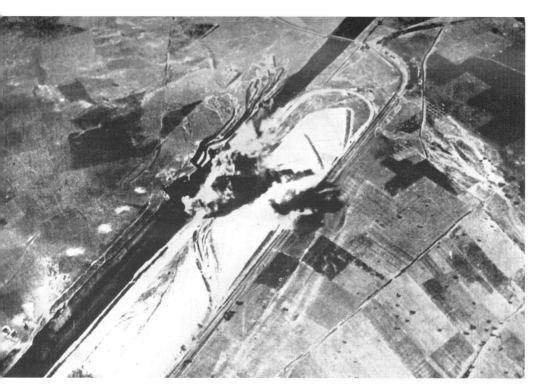

A dramatic aerial photograph showing an attack by the Italians against the Corinth Canal, which links the Ionian and Aegean seas.

The aircraft carrier HMS *Ark Royal* under fire from Italian forces in the Mediterranean.

Blackburn Skua dive-bombers on the deck of HMS *Ark Royal*.

Light anti-submarine bombs aboard a Bristol Blenheim of Coastal Command, undergoing a final check before going out on patrol.

Right: Bristol Beauforts of Coastal Command on patrol over the sea.

Below: A Coastal Command crew compares notes after returning to base from a long patrol at sea.

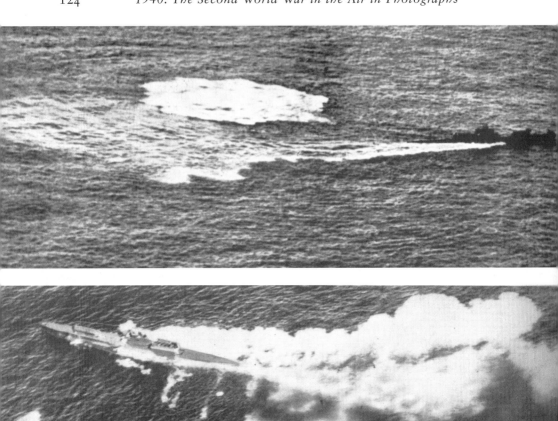

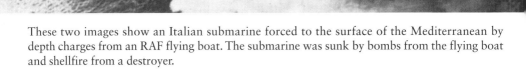

These two images show an Italian submarine forced to the surface of the Mediterranean by depth charges from an RAF flying boat. The submarine was sunk by bombs from the flying boat and shellfire from a destroyer.

Another way to fight the U-boat menace. This artist's impression shows a Hampden bomber laying mines at the entrance to an enemy submarine base. Missions like this were known by the codename 'Gardening'.

Bombed invasion barges ashore on the French coast following an attack by the RAF. A freighter can be seen listing in the background.

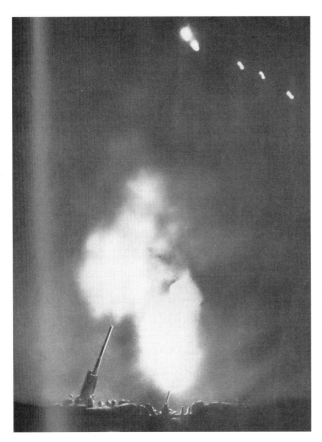

Left: Anti-aircraft guns fire at raiders during the night, while flares can be seen falling at the top right of the photograph.

Below: A classic image of the Blitz: the dome of St Paul's Cathedral rises up out of the smoke of the fires all around it on the night of 29 December 1940.

Right: Firefighters in the streets of the City of London on the night of 29 December.

Below: Winston Churchill, accompanied by his wife Clementine, tours the areas of London damaged in the raids of 29 December.

Another view of St Paul's Cathedral, through the remaining structure of a bombed-out building the morning after the great raid of 29 December.